The Guiding Light of a Grandmother's Love

The Return of
Happy Harper
Thursdays

Written by Fern Schumer Chapman

Illustrated by Phoebe Chandler Turner

Published February 1, 2021, by Gussie Rose Press, Lake Bluff, Illinois

Book design by Lorie DeWorken.

ISBN: 978-0-9964725-8-6 (paperback)
ISBN: 978-0-9964725-9-3 (ebook)

Library of Congress Cataloguing-in-Publication Data:
    Chapman, Fern Schumer
    Turner, Phoebe Chandler
    The Return of Happy Harper Thursdays by Fern Schumer Chapman, Illustrated by Phoebe Chandler Turner
    ISBN:
    1. Unconditional love 2. Grandparents 3. Grandchildren 4. Family separation 5. Social distancing 6. Coronavirus – social aspects
        7. Bibliotherapy for children 8. Children and emotional intelligence

For Keith Chapman,
who inspired this story

I last saw you months and months ago.

No matter how you count it
– by seasons, weeks, or days –
it's been way too long.

Now, doctors have a vaccine
– a kind of medicine –
that makes sure people won't get sick.

The nasty bug is leaving town,
and we can finally be together!

As I drive to your house, I wonder:
How much have you grown?

Is your pretty red hair long enough for a ponytail?

What new games will we play?

Why does the road to your house seem so long today?

When I get there, I know you'll jump into my arms
and hug me tight. You'll never want to let me go.

I *vroom-vroom* the car to get to you faster!

At last, I'm knocking on your door.
I call to you, "Harper! Hi!" But you don't look up.

"I'm so happy to see you!" I say.
But you just keep pouring tea for Dolly and Snickers.

I pull up a tiny chair to your table.
"Will you pour me a cup of tea, please?"

"Harper, are you mad at me?"

This is *not* how I thought things would go!

"I have something for you in my purse."

Finally, you look up.
There it is: a small smile starting.

"I *wanted* to visit you, Harper," I say.
"I've been sad, too."

"We missed so many Thursdays together.
We could have been collecting pinecones...."

"And watching robins build their nests..."

"And picking daffodils for your mom."

"But we're together now! Here, this is for you."

I hope we'll never have to skip our
Happy Harper Thursdays again. But if we do,
this picture will help you remember."

"Even when you can't see me, Harper...

"My love for you is a light that's always on."

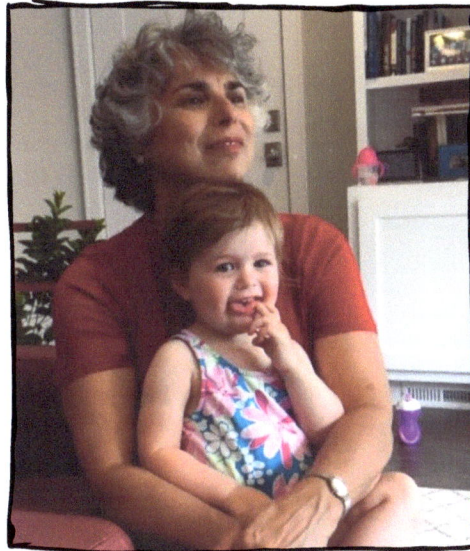

Fern Schumer Chapman (a.k.a."Mama Fern") is a grandmother of Harper and baby Dylan Edith. She is an award-winning author of several books, including *Happy Harper Thursdays*, *Motherland*, and *Is it Night or Day?*.

For more information about her work, please visit
http://fernschumerchapman.com

Phoebe Chandler Turner is a grandmother of two and an illustrator.

The two friends and neighbors collaborated on the "Happy Harper" series while respecting social distancing during the 2020-2021 Coronavirus shelter-in-place restrictions.